HE.
GIRL,
HE
SEES
YOU

KELLY FAULKENBERY

A wholly owned subsidiary of **T B N**

Hey Girl, He Sees You
Trilogy Christian Publishers
A Wholly Owned Subsidiary of Trinity Broadcasting Network
2442 Michelle Drive
Tustin, CA 92780

For information, address Trilogy Christian Publishing
Rights Department, 2442 Michelle Drive, Tustin, CA 92780.

For information about special discounts for bulk purchases, please contact Trilogy Christian Publishing.
Manufactured in the United States of America

10 9 8 7 6 5 4 3 2 1
Library of Congress Cataloging-in-Publication Data is available.
ISBN: 978-1-68556-579-4
ISBN: 978-1-68556-580-0

DEDICATION

This book is dedicated to my husband, Corbett. Thank you for being on the adventure over these twenty-seven years. I love that you love Jesus, love my balloon floating, and that you encourage me to finish strong and see this dream into a reality. This is only the beginning, and I am so ready for the next chapter of our lives.

To my kids- Garrett, Cameron, Logan, and Payton- you each have my heart. You are my inspiration. Live passionately, pursue your dreams, and always keep Jesus at the center of it all.

ACKNOWLEDGMENTS

I would be remiss if I did not mention my tribe. Stephanie, Sooz, and Amanda- thank you for each always encouraging a dreamer, for being there through life's ups and downs, and being willing to get on board the adventure train. I am not sure where we will end up but if we are all on board with coffee, pie, and Jesus there is no other adventure I would rather be on!

Pastor Molly- thank you for your friendship. My gratitude for your words of encouragement, your prayers, meetings, and discussions even when they were hard will always be treasured. Thank you for believing in the dreams and visions and guiding me through the journey.

Pastor Ryan-What to say besides I am eternally grateful for your friendship, guidance, and encouragement not just for me but our whole family. Thank you for being such a wonderful example of being His hands and feet. I am living in expectation; expecting God in every situation, every area of our lives and trusting His timing, living in an overflow of His love.

Michael Russo, my heart turned upside down and listened like it had never heard the Word. Your obedience caused my heart and eyes to be opened to see heaven. Thank you, I and our generations are eternally grateful.

PREFACE

Identity is something I struggled with for years. *Who am I?* is a question many of us ask ourselves yet are we truly ready to find. I know I have many labels in life that identify different roles I lead in this crazy journey of life: daughter, wife, mother to three boys and one girl, friend, co-worker, boss lady, the list could go on and on. In my younger years, the list was different, yet I struggled to be the best at whatever the label was for the given season. In fact, I was good at trying to achieve the perfection that these labels defined me in each season to the point that these roles and labels became chains. The chains were heavy. The struggle to juggle all of them and life and perform distracted me from well...me! I lost myself, my purpose, my desire to thrive, dream or pursue passions. The feelings of inadequacy and failure began to blur lines in my reality and before I knew it, I was filling this hole in my soul with everything the world was demanding me to be instead of walking in who I am. Ever been there? Lost, confused, exhausted, and looked over.

The biggest game the enemy has out there are two things in my opinion: distraction and deception. I believe women tend to, in general, be more "feelers" than our counterparts and if we listen to the world, and all the noise out there, we fall into the same trap I did and begin to believe the lies of distraction and deception. Let me give you a few examples: "You are not good enough, you can't do that, girls don't do that, that dream is sill, that won't support you or a family, it just doesn't make sense, you need to lose weight, maybe if you were more like_____, if I could be a mom like her maybe my home would be happier, maybe if I dressed like that or looked like her." etc. etc. Then, and only then, would my problems dissolve and I would have what it takes. I lived in comparing your outsides to my insides. Then I would super study your outsides like what you did, how you talk, how you cook, or dress or would listen for others accolades about you and then implement a plan to be that person. After all, I was comparing my insides to your outsides that seems right, right? By the end of what I call the chameleon season, I was lost, tired and empty down to the depths of my soul and was questioning what in the whole wide world I was doing here anyway and what God would want with someone like me.

There is hope! This book is to break chains of all the labels to break off the chameleon season to open your eyes, ears, and to fill the hole in your soul with all God is speaking to you so that you can embrace this adventure. God is calling you to a life far bigger than you could ever dream or imagine. Join me on a journey to embark upon the adventure of a lifetime that sets you free to embrace the love of the Father who is calling you to draw near. This is not for the faint of heart, there will be tears and it may sting a little pulling off a band-aid, but I promise if you are willing to risk it all, chains will fall, lies and strongholds will be broken, and a new freedom and an unmatched all-encompassing love affair awaits with the One who calls you Beloved.

INTRODUCTION

Welcome to a journey that will take you to new depths in your relationship with Christ! I'm so glad that you're here with me! As you go through this workbook, we're going to dive deep into identity, connection, and encounter.

Identity will play a big role in our work throughout. You'll hear me talk a lot about labels. This is important to discuss because who we think we are defines what we do. Our society insists on labeling everything and sometimes we can adopt some that prevent us from fully living out our calling. It's my hope that we can look at these things together and get rid of ones that hold us back.

Connection is key! Every woman needs a tribe, and I pray you can find one in your work throughout this book. Some women choose to do this study in the company of other women, and some choose to do it alone. Whatever route you take, I hope you can bring boldness into the vulnerability and transparency to be you, the real you to the women in your closest (inner) circle.

Encounter is maybe the most pivotal aspect of this workbook. It's designed to bring about a deep and fulfilling relationship with Christ through introspection, admission, and prayer. When we fill our lives with stuff that doesn't matter, it's because we're really searching for a spiritual connection. In fact, a spiritual connection is truly all that sustains us now and will continue to sustain us for years to come. We all seek joy, and we find it in a life-changing encounter with Christ – no matter how long we've been in church.

But before we get too far into it, let me give you a little lay o' the land so you know what to expect.

In the first two parts, we're going to look at the labels and obstacles for some figures from the Bible. This is good for us because we get to see how even when the struggle is real, God is present, merciful, and loving. Then in parts three and four, we take it to a new level. You will be called to see yourself as He sees you and begin to embrace your new identity. Finally, in parts five and six, we take our precious discoveries and look at how to launch out into everyday living!

With our new-found passions and armed with all God says we are and all He's leading us to be, we look into everyday applications of living out our royal callings as daughters of the King!

Each part has the following format:

Introduction

Scripture - Sword

Engage & Unleash

Chain Breakers

Awaken & Arise

The Introduction and Scripture sections give you the lay of the land for the upcoming journey you will embark upon as you dive into all God has to reveal to you in each section. As you dive in deeper throughout the lesson, there is scripture strategically placed for you to pick up your sword and prepare to run to the battle and break the chains that are holding you back from embracing your true identity and living the life the Creator of the universe designed for you! Ephesians 6:13, MSG says the following, "Be prepared. You're up against far more than you can handle on your own. Take all the help you can get, every weapon God has issued, so that when it's all over but the shouting you'll still be on your feet. Truth, righteousness, peace, faith, and salvation are more than words. Learn how to apply them. You'll need them throughout your life. God's Word is an indispensable weapon."

Engage & Unleash is the place where you get to take all that we just discussed and hash it out. This is where we get to get real and get down to unveiling the lies, and the chains that are keeping you from you. I am giving you opportunities to get real and put yourself out there. This is a roll up your sleeves and go all in moment designed to take you deeper into you. You can share with others or keep this between you and God. This is where, if you risk it all, you find the real you. Watch out world, the lioness inside you is unleashed!

Chain Breakers have been written to do just that- break chains! I want you to find a mirror in your home or your car etc. and look at yourself and declare boldly the chain breaker for each section. Repeating these chain breakers, daily, empower you to walk in your true identity. Your words matter. As the old saying goes, the pen is mightier than the sword, scripture states in Proverbs 12:18, "There is one whose rash words are like sword thrusts, but the tongue of the wise brings healing." So, ladies, you are going to find your voice and embrace Truth all while we speak it out loud over ourselves because yes, your words matter and yes you matter! I want to hear you speaking love and light over yourself every day and you too will hear those chains fallin'...I do and oh what a joyful noise it is to hear the clanging as they fall away!

After you hear the chains falling, you will embark upon Awaken & Arise. This is to get your armor on and go all in as you take risk in real time (faith=risk). A call to action in this section will stir your soul and move you into a shifting of how you see the world, how you interact with the worlds around you, my dear one, will reveal the true you. It's where the decision is made weekly to get on the field and run to the battle or remain safely chained to the bench. You get to make the choice. I have laid out some challenges in front of you hoping and contending for you, yes you, to awaken and arise!

It's my hope that you'll be challenged by this journey. Yes, it'll be hard to slough off old labels, look at burdens, and awaken to new truth. No one ever said that's an easy job, and if they did, they're lying. If you're participating in this journey with a group of women, I hope you can connect with one another as this provides a safe area to truly dialog about thoughts and feelings that come as you dive into your identity. It can be scary being vulnerable! This is a place to be totally real and completely raw. Hard conversations help set us free and launch us into all we are called and created to be! Can I get a woohoo?!

I've also included parts of my own story to help you connect with the material we discuss. Without letting the cat out of the bag in the introduction, I'll just let you know I left the family pew and found a few comfortable haunts in life's gutter. I didn't wear pearls; I didn't fit in with the church folk; I was a loud, drunk black sheep. If you identify as one of these, welcome! If you're appalled at my open admission, welcome! No matter what your background is, you're going to learn something.

Come on, y'all! The adventure train is calling! Let's get going!

PART I

Who Are You?

Therefore, if anyone is in Christ, he is a new creation.
The old has passed away; behold, the new has come.
2 Corinthians 5:17 (MSG)

The hour before the sun rises is an interesting time. I'm an early bird, so I've seen this hour a lot. It's still dark outside, but there's just a little light peeking between the trees. Shadows are everywhere and it's hard to see where you're going. As the sun wakes up, everything outside begins to change.

I lived a long time in the hour before sunrise. I was raised in a Lutheran house. Everything had its proper place. Mom would dress me up in dresses she made that coordinated with my brother's outfits, plaid and all. In perfect 70s fashion, she'd curl my hair to get just the right look, even if it meant an accidental burn for the sake of perfection. People at church admired our put-togetherness. We were an ideal looking family, like, Saturday Evening Post ideal. What they never saw was me scratching at every inch of skin I could because my mom's dress was an uncomfortable, but pretty, straight jacket, and my ear still burned from where she burned me with the curling iron.

As I got older in the church, I began to feel more and more that I didn't fit in somehow. I remember talking to the pastor of my church, proudly telling him that someday I wanted to grow up to be a pastor. With a swift and calculated comment, he dashed all those hopes in one fail swoop. "Girls don't become pastors. You can shine the silver for communion, or you can teach Sunday school, but you can't become a pastor because girls don't do that." By this time in my life, I began to have visions and hear God speaking to me, leading me towards something bigger. I thought I was following that call. You can imagine that I was wholly and holy confused when this spiritual man I looked up to told me that God didn't have a place for me there. That's what he thought, but not what He thought.

I eventually made the jump from private school to wild public school. In my switch, where I went from Jesus every day all week to Jesus on Wednesdays and Sundays, I started getting all the wrong kinds of attention. Something in me started to lash out at the confusion and the fear. I acted out. I gained the notice of the principal. I made friends who were also scared and lashed out. I began to live and breathe in a shadowland. Fear made me put on masks, go places I didn't want to, and act in this strange, foreign way. And the shadowland didn't just magically appear. It crept in slowly until it was everywhere around me.

Because I couldn't see, I became very good at being

whoever I thought the people around me wanted me to be, so good, in fact, that I got lost. I was the chameleon in the jungle -- ever changing to avoid detection. I said what I thought you wanted me to say, did what I thought you wanted me to do, even felt how I thought you wanted me to feel -- all so that I could win the affection and acceptance of the world and avoid the pain of rejection. I didn't like or accept myself. To comprehend the supernatural love and acceptance I already had was a long way off for me.

Yes, I knew of God and His word and knew that He was good, but I didn't know who I was or what in the world I was supposed to be doing. I had a head full of knowledge and a heart empty and desperate for a relationship. I could quote scripture. I could tell you a lot about the Word, more than most kids, I guess. But hearing and reading about God's love is different from experiencing and comprehending God's love. I've read that nature hates a vacuum, and so the empty space that was created because I distanced myself from the only sustainable source of power began to fill with trash of all kinds. This hole in my soul collected different things the world told me would make me happy: relationships, accolades, alcohol, drugs, clothes, friendships, material possessions, the approval of others. I became an overachiever. Whatever I did, I was going to do so good that you'd love me and accept me. Yet, even with achievements and worldly successes I was empty, hurting, and estranged from God and family. So, so, so estranged.

I got married to a man who loved to drink as much as me. I went to church off and on with my parents, but always with some invisible cloud of shame hung over my head. I felt each time I entered those doors that I had the scarlet letter written all over me. I had so many labels for myself: bad, broken, worthless, insignificant, incapable, black sheep, drunk, chaotic child, too much, a mess. When I got divorced only eight months after getting married and moved in with my parents, I continued to go to church to appease them – now with another label. I didn't know who I really was outside of these labels. I had shapeshifted for so long that who God made me to be had been lost in the pursuit of worldly love. I had my labels, and that was all I had.

I desperately wanted to be loved. I wanted more than anything to avoid pain and rejection. I sacrificed principles willingly if it meant I could keep away from feeling unwanted. But this only separated me more from my purpose. It enslaved me, and I had been the one who laced up my own chains.

That's just part of my story. The rest is for later.

Maybe you've felt this way, too. Maybe you've worn your own scarlet letter. Maybe you've come up wanting after seeking knowledge instead of a relationship. Maybe you've felt unworthy, and maybe you've been too afraid to say it out loud. Let's take a look at a figure from the Bible who struggled with the same things.

Ah, the Old Testament. Turn to Genesis 16 (MSG) and let's look at the story of Hagar.

16 1-2 Sarai, Abram's wife, hadn't yet produced a child. She had an Egyptian maid named Hagar. Sarai said to Abram, "God has not seen fit to let me have a child. Sleep with my maid. Maybe I can get a family from her." Abram agreed to do what Sarai said.

3-4 So Sarai, Abram's wife, took her Egyptian maid Hagar and gave her to her husband Abram as a wife. Abram had been living ten years in Canaan when this took place. He slept with Hagar, and she got pregnant. When Hagar learned she was pregnant, she looked down on her mistress.

5 Sarai told Abram, "It's all your fault that I'm suffering this abuse. I put my maid in bed with you and the minute she knows she's pregnant, she treats me like I'm nothing. May God decide which of us is right."

6 "You decide," said Abram. "Your maid is your business." Sarai was abusive to Hagar and Hagar ran away.

7-8 An angel of God found her beside a spring in the desert; it was the spring on the road to Shur. He said, "Hagar, maid of Sarai, what are you doing here?" She said, "I'm running away from Sarai, my mistress."

9-12 The angel of God said, "Go back to your mistress. Put up with her abuse." He continued, "I'm going to give you a big family, children past counting. From this pregnancy, you'll get a son: Name him Ishmael; for God heard you, God answered you. He'll be a bucking bronco of a man, a real fighter, fighting and being fought, always stirring up trouble, always at odds with his family."

13 She answered God by name, praying to the God who spoke to her, "You're the God who sees me! "Yes! He saw me; and then I saw him!"

14 That's how that desert spring got named "God-Alive-Sees-Me Spring." That spring is still there, between Kadesh and Bered.

15-16 Hagar gave Abram a son. Abram named him Ishmael. Abram was eighty-six years old when Hagar gave him his son, Ishmael.

Woah, woah, woah! This is a major drama moment! If you're like me, you might've seen Hagar as a straight up homewrecker. She's usually looked at as a troublemaker for Sarai, a well-respected womanly figure. See the labels?

Picture this: a young, beautiful woman who probably

had great skin and no gray hair. She doesn't have any kids, so she probably had time to actually brush her hair and wear makeup and definitely didn't have any baby spit on her dress. And then she went off and slept with another woman's husband. We have an immediate dislike for her. No way! Shame on her! Stone her!

But hang on. Before we stone her in the streets, let's look at few facts:

- Sarai gave her to Abraham.
- Hagar had Sarai's trust as a servant.
- Hagar was obedient.

As you read in Genesis 16, you'll find Hagar really does have it rough and was treated unfairly by Sarai. She was overworked and beat and turned every which way from the right way. I'm sure she felt just as lost as we do sometimes. Eventually, she fled into a harsh land with her son, Ishmael. Maybe we have some sympathy for her. She went from having a good job and some measure of security to being alone and abandoned by the people she had sought the approval of. But God -- Yes, God! -- made a promise to Hagar and was faithful to her because of her obedience. God knew her actions. God was faithful anyway.

Think about the labels the world put on her: homewrecker, snake, broken, sick. Those would definitely not go on her resume. But what labels do you think Hagar had given herself? Failure, mistake-maker, lost, misguided, weak. Sometimes the labels we give ourselves are far more damaging than the ones given by those around us. I know I labeled myself after doing a few unbiblical things and they never did serve me well.

Bring It In!

The world gave Hagar an identity. We can see how she was affected by this identity, too. God's Word tells us who we really are, and sometimes the world's noise crowds this truth out. It's our job to look at these things in the light. It's our job to take the hand of Jesus so He can lead us into a new place, one where we embrace who He created us to be -- no matter what our previous or current sins. We must accurately and fearlessly call out these labels. Then we must cast them to the side. When we nurture the fire of this truth, we are lit up from the inside out!

_____

_____

_____

_____

_____

_____

_____

_____

_____

_____

_____

_____

Engage & Unleash

Write down five to ten labels you or the world has given you (these can be positive or negative).

_____

_____

_____

_____

_____

_____

_____

_____

_____

_____

_____

_____

_____

_____

_____

_____

_____

_____

_____

_____

_____

_____

Ask a loved one or friend this week to give you three words that describe you.

_____

_____

_____

_____

_____

_____

_____

_____

_____

_____

_____

_____

_____

_____

_____

_____

_____

_____

_____

_____

_____

_____

WHO ARE YOU

In your quiet time, ask God what words He uses to describe you.

_____

_____

_____

_____

_____

_____

_____

_____

_____

_____

_____

_____

_____

_____

_____

_____

_____

_____

_____

_____

_____

_____

_____

_____

Write a paragraph introducing yourself to a women's group as if no one in the group knows you.

_____

_____

_____

_____

_____

_____

_____

_____

_____

_____

_____

_____

_____

_____

_____

_____

_____

_____

_____

_____

_____

_____

_____

WHO ARE YOU

Write a paragraph introducing yourself to Jesus. Did your paragraph need to change from the previous one you wrote? Why?

_____

_____

_____

_____

_____

_____

_____

_____

_____

_____

_____

_____

_____

_____

_____

_____

_____

_____

_____

_____

_____

_____

_____

_____

WHO ARE YOU

_____

_____

_____

_____

_____

_____

_____

_____

_____

_____

_____

_____

_____

_____

_____

_____

_____

_____

_____

_____

_____

_____

_____

_____

_____

_____

_____

_____

Chain Breakers:

I am worthy!

I am His!

God loves me and makes me new every day!

I am a light, and I will shine bright for the world to see!

Awaken & Arise

Have you ever been looked upon as a troublemaker? Have you ever been wrongly accused? What about the other side of that: have you ever been the accuser? Whether we realize it or not, being labeled by others or assigning labels to people we don't like affects our relationship with people and with God. Think about one or two people who fit into those categories: they were your accuser, or you were theirs. Make a commitment to pray blessings for them over the next two weeks. In the beginning, these may feel insincere. It sometimes takes a few days for the Spirit to change our hearts! That's okay! Continue to pray for them until you have a new revelation. It'll come. Trust me.

PART II

What Blocks You?

"When she heard about Jesus, she came up behind him in the crowd and touched his cloak, because she thought, If I just touch his clothes, I will be healed.*"*
Mark 5:27-28 (MSG)

If what goes up must come down, then what goes down must also come up. I might be off on the physics of that scenario, but you get my drift. God shines His light in the darkness, so without darkness we can't reveal His glory. And despite many of us wanting an easy way through, there is usually some resistance when we begin to "make our way through the crowd" to find Jesus. So, we have to look at what holds us back and how to push through to encounter Him. I remember what happened when I surrendered and took a risk and believed that maybe Jesus had room for someone like me! Let's look at two women in the Bible who, in the midst of the hurt and shame, surrendered and broke through the barriers that stood between them and a new life because they realized who God said they were.

The Unclean Woman

We'll begin in Mark 5:25-34, MSG, and look at the woman with the issue of blood. This woman wasn't out in the great big world living her best life. Nay! She was absolutely suffering for years. Because she was considered unclean, she was alone and likely felt totally unwanted by everyone who knew her. No touch from family or partner – only the greedy touch of "healers" who were hellbent on taking what money she had. Imagine this life for her day in and day out – all the same, all quiet, all a tunnel of struggle. No one wanted to be around her, and in a world where women are the underdog, you can only imagine her years of conflict and how weary she must have been.

> 25-29 A woman who had suffered a condition of hemorrhaging for twelve years—a long succession of physicians had treated her, and treated her badly, taking all her money and leaving her worse off than before— had heard about Jesus. She slipped in from behind and touched his robe. She was thinking to herself, "If I can put a finger on his robe, I can get well." The moment she did it, the flow of blood dried up. She could feel the change and knew her plague was over and done with.

> 30 At the same moment, Jesus felt energy discharging from him. He turned around to the crowd and asked, "Who touched my robe?"

31 His disciples said, "What are you talking about? With this crowd pushing and jostling you, you're asking, 'Who touched me?' Dozens have touched you!"

32-33 But he went on asking, looking around to see who had done it. The woman, knowing what had happened, knowing she was the one, stepped up in fear and trembling, knelt before him, and gave him the whole story.

34 Jesus said to her, "Daughter, you took a risk of faith, and now you're healed and whole. Live well, live blessed! Be healed of your plague."

Our unclean woman was surrounded by people in the crowd. Jesus was a way off from her, and to get to Him she was going to have to work. Her struggle was real. She had to wade, duck, dodge, wiggle, and squeeze through people to get close enough to touch the hem of his garment. She wasn't mesmerized by the first brush of skin from someone in the crowd. She was fixated on the Teacher, the Master, the Healer. She didn't give up even though I'm sure people continued to move in her way. She didn't let stigma stop her. She forgot, even for just a moment, the labels she had been given by others and herself because her only thought was on how Jesus could make her new. She fought past distractions, the opinions of others, fear, and weariness from years being alone. She had faith, and that faith carried her through until she was able to fall on the ground and get one finger on the clothes He wore.

The Adulteress Woman

This is one of my favorites found in Luke 7:36-50, MSG. An adulterous woman comes to a dinner party that she had not been invited to.....wait, what? Let's read that again: an adulteress woman (gasp!) comes to a dinner party (bigger gasp!) that she had not been invited to (biggest gasp!). Let's look at the Word again. This woman, this adulterous woman (her label) was broken, undone, and overwhelmed with shame and guilt. She definitely wasn't rolling in with her head up. If I were to guess, she probably couldn't stand herself anymore. But she was willing to risk it all to be near Jesus! She found a way into this party full of people who she knew didn't like her, had just enough desperation to sit in the room with the people she knew didn't like her, and then didn't run when I'm sure she felt the urge to escape all the dagger eyes.

36-39 One of the Pharisees asked him over for a meal. He went to the Pharisee's house and sat down at the dinner table. Just then a woman of the village, the town harlot, having learned that Jesus was a guest in the home of the Pharisee, came with a bottle of very expensive perfume and stood at his feet, weeping, raining tears on his feet. Letting down her hair, she dried his feet, kissed them, and anointed them with the perfume. When the Pharisee who had invited him saw this, he said to himself, "If this man was the prophet I thought he was, he would have known what kind of woman this is who is falling all over him."

40 Jesus said to him, "Simon, I have something to tell you."

"Oh? Tell me."

41-42 "Two men were in debt to a banker. One owed five hundred silver pieces, the other fifty. Neither of them could pay up, and so the banker canceled both debts. Which of the two would be more grateful?"

43-47 Simon answered, "I suppose the one who was forgiven the most."

"That's right," said Jesus. Then turning to the woman, but speaking to Simon, he said, "Do you see this woman? I came to your home; you provided no water for my feet, but she rained tears on my feet and dried them with her hair. You gave me no greeting, but from the time I arrived she hasn't quit kissing my feet. You provided nothing for freshening up, but she has soothed my feet with perfume. Impressive, isn't it? She was forgiven many, many sins, and so she is very, very grateful. If the forgiveness is minimal, the gratitude is minimal."

48 Then he spoke to her: "I forgive your sins."

49 That set the dinner guests talking behind his back: "Who does he think he is, forgiving sins!"

50 He ignored them and said to the woman, "Your faith has saved you. Go in peace."

She proved herself determined, desperate, and hungry. She fought past her own shame, threw off her label, and ignored the opinions of others, all so she could sit at the feet of Jesus. Make no mistake. For both her and the unclean woman, this was an act of will.

For both of these women, their labels were clear to them. Society in biblical times didn't coddle anyone. No one had any sensitivity training. If you were marked in a negative way, you were an outcast, and your life unfolded the way an outcast's would. Labels were as relevant then as they are now. These labels affected these women, and they were aware of them for sure. Despite this, they found a way to unchain themselves.

Have you ever felt unclean? Unworthy? The woman in the book of Mark had suffered silently for a long time, and society told her there was nothing she was worthy of because she and everything she touched was unclean. Did she ask for this illness? Did she blame God? Had she sought help? There was no treatment or cure, and so she was left alone. Life handed her a big bag of lemons and there was hardly a way to make lemonade. What are your moments of feeling alone? When have people told you to go away? When have you felt rejected or unwanted?

When I was living and breathing and then completely drowning in addiction, nothing about my life was clean. It can't be if you want to survive in those circumstances. And it is a lonely disease. Not only did the outside world look at me as someone who people shouldn't be around, I felt the same way about who I was. I tried long and hard to escape myself but couldn't shake the mental and physical torture. Yes, I was suffering from a physical illness -- an addiction that had me in its grip and wouldn't let go. I didn't just feel alone. I was alone. I didn't just feel unclean. I was unclean. In that dark hour before dawn, I didn't blame God, but I didn't call on Him either. My self-loathing, my feeling of unworthiness, my shame kept me outside the crowd of people, outside the dinner party where I was surely an unwanted guest. And this shame kept me chained to my addiction for a long time.

Let's go back to the adulterous woman who made her way into this party. The woman knows she is unwelcomed and that the consequences of her actions could be severe, yet she found a way to Jesus. She showed us how to go after Him, despite our sin, despite the labels given to us by others and ourselves, despite everything. She was likely snickered at, spit on, whispered about, but she made the trudge. How are you like the woman at the party? What barriers are you willing to walk through to get to Jesus? When have you shown determination in life? What did others say about you when you were pushing through? Did you believe lies, or did you keep going after your goal?

When the woman gets to His feet, she lets it all go. I believe at this monumental moment, it's just her and her Savior. She can't see any of those other people in the room, and she is completely and utterly undone and present in the moment. The nearer we are to Jesus, the more freedom we experience.

Bring It In!

Go to the mirror and take a long look. Who do you see? Describe yourself: all your physical features, feelings, and thoughts. Think about your story and leave nothing out: all your struggles, your feelings amidst those struggles, the moments where you questioned and felt unworthy, and your moments of celebration. Tell yourself your story – speak these things out loud. The adulteress woman and the unclean woman have had the same struggles. The details of their stories and your story might be different, but the main conflict is the same: we need and long for a deep and fulfilling encounter with our Savior, and we have obstacles when we seek that encounter.

WHAT BLOCKS YOU

Engage & Unleash

Take all your resentments, struggles, fears, heaviness, and past sin and write them all down. This is just for you to see unless you decide to share it with someone. I know this can be overwhelming and painful. It's like dragging a rake along the bottom of a muddy river. This can begin to cloud your thoughts and take over your emotions. No matter what, fight through this and make your way to Jesus.

_____

_____

_____

_____

_____

_____

_____

_____

_____

_____

_____

_____

_____

_____

_____

_____

_____

_____

_____

WHAT BLOCKS YOU

When you're done, take a moment and look at this list, then tear it out of your journal. Get in a quiet space with God. Go to Him and sit at His feet like the woman. Sit with Him and lay your list at His feet -- all of it: the struggles, the secrets, the sins, the labels. Complete surrender. When you're ready, say this prayer:

"Jesus, come and give me a word, a verse, a picture of who you say I am. I am willing to push through a crowd to get to You. I am willing to lay down what I think I know about myself and what the world has said about me, in favor of knowing what You think about me. I pray for the truth. I pray for light. I pray for Your will for me. Amen."

Come back to this prayer as often as you need or want. It's not a bad idea to write it down on a sticky note and put it on your mirror!

Chain Breakers:

I am a child of God!

I am beautifully and wonderfully made. Jesus loves me and I am His favorite!

I am loved, treasured, and am worthy of goodness and love- His amazing perfect love

Awaken & Arise

This week as you made a list of past hurts, labels, and chains you were to lay them at Jesus's feet. Grab a new sheet of paper and sit with Jesus and write down what you see or draw a picture. Don't worry about what it looks like as far as artistic abilities, stick figures are my artsy side, but be completely open to all you see, all you feel, all you small, all you hear. Write this down. You may want to continue this exercise for a few days in a row this week and at the end see what is consistent and what is new. You can do it; I hear chains falling and smell the sweet sweet aroma of heaven coming down over you. You can do this; you are His beloved. Make your way all the way, sit all the way down, touch His feet and stay.

_____

_____

_____

_____

_____

_____

_____

_____

_____

_____

_____

_____

_____

WHAT BLOCKS YOU

PART III

Who Does Jesus See?

But God demonstrates his own love for us in this: While we were still sinners, Christ died for us.
Romans 5:8 (MSG)

By this time in our journey, we've taken a look at some hard truths and have done what we can to lay them all down because they no longer serve us. We have shed light on our desperation for an encounter. We've probably laughed and cried. We've definitely found ourselves vulnerable.

At the end of my active alcoholism, I found myself at my most desperate. I had tried so many things to get the voices in my head to stop, to get my skin to fit right, and nothing lasted. In my darkest moment, I made the decision to empty the whole medicine cabinet into my stomach and wash it down with all the alcohol in the house. I came out of unconsciousness in the hospital to the face of the same preacher I had seen so many times before. My attempt to tell God, "I quit!" had failed. It was the beginning of the end.

This is the moment that led me to a 12-step group where people who felt like me came together in the same room to talk about how they overcame terrible monsters. They were riffraff! Some of them smoked, some of them cussed, some of them still didn't shower regularly, but they all spoke about how God, as they understood Him, had done for them what they couldn't do for themselves. As a proud black sheep, this comforted me. It appeared I found my tribe.

I hope you're starting to feel a little lighter, and if you're not, don't worry. Buckle up, buttercup! In this section we are going to dig into what Jesus says about us and that He calls us His even when we mess up. The idea that God loved me in spite of my own mistakes was a complete and total game changer for me. Yes, Jesus loves us even after all our indiscretions and past failures, and even with a laundry list of decisions that we wouldn't want advertised on our social media, He calls us Beloved. Period. End of story. This became more and more true the more I listened and talked to those people who had been in the gutter like me. From then on, I knew I was forever changed and completely sold-out to Him all my days. Let's look at another unlikely nobody from the Bible and their game changing moment: Zacchaeus. Ah, good ol', slimy Zacchaeus. Luke 19:1-10 tells the story of a short, grubby tax collector who was collectively disliked by probably everyone who met him. Taxes haven't gained in popularity in the last several thousand years, so you can imagine the vibe Zacchaeus gave to people. And not only was he basically an ancient IRS employee, but he was also known for taking extra money for himself in addition to the Roman tax that was to be collected. Nobody, and I mean nobody, was inviting Zacchaeus to dinner. In the middle of all his stealing in the name of the Emperor, he caught wind of Jesus coming to town. He'd heard lots about this Jesus guy and wanted to see him, too – but remember, he was short and hated. Must have been easy for him to find a spot in the crowd. NOPE. Lots of people wanted to see Jesus, and no one in that crowd along the street was going to let bozo Zacchaeus in.

People couldn't say he was dumb though. He ran and climbed high into a tree so he could see Jesus walk by. As He passed him, and to everyone's shock, Jesus called to Zacchaeus, who was elated to be seen. Despite whom Zacchaeus was and what he had done, Jesus went to this tax collector's house for dinner.

Wait, what?

Why would Jesus choose this house and this type of person to hang with? It didn't make sense to anyone in town why the Savior of the world would pick dumb Zacchaeus to spend time with. There were many good-hearted people in the crowd, many people who did the right thing consistently, many who most would call worthy of such an honor. But Jesus saw Zacchaeus's heart. Jesus sees our hearts. In his home, Zacchaeus had an encounter with the love and acceptance of Jesus that completely changed his cold, tax-collecting heart. He had a complete surrender.

He had an overwhelming, life-changing experience not because his story made him worthy, but because the story Jesus had for him was.

Bring It In!

I've had an opportunity to fly all over the country sharing my story with others who suffer from the same disease I have. From hospital beds to podiums on stage, God saw my story, my mistakes, my darkness, and He called me because of these things. If it weren't for my mistakes, I wouldn't have a victory to share. Those victories give hope to hundreds and thousands of people. This is what God saw in me. He saw my heart. He saw me for who I truly am. When I came into the light, the darkness I experienced turned out to be one of my biggest tools for bringing light to others. God doesn't love us because of what we do; He loves us because we are His – mess and all. He truly does have a plan for us.

_____

_____

_____

_____

_____

_____

_____

_____

_____

_____

WHO DOES JESUS SEE?

Engage & Unleash

Reflect on your relationship with Jesus now. Are you in relationship with Him? Do you love sitting with Him? Does it feel awkward at times? Are there things you still don't understand? Write about these.

_____

_____

_____

_____

_____

_____

_____

_____

_____

_____

_____

_____

_____

_____

_____

_____

_____

_____

_____

_____

_____

_____

_____

WHO DOES JESUS SEE?

_____

_____

_____

_____

_____

_____

_____

_____

_____

_____

_____

_____

_____

_____

_____

_____

_____

_____

_____

_____

_____

_____

_____

_____

_____

_____

_____

Do you have a "Come-Out-Of-The-Tree" moment like Zacchaeus had? If your answer is no, what do you think is holding you back?

_____

_____

_____

_____

_____

_____

_____

_____

_____

_____

_____

_____

_____

_____

_____

_____

_____

_____

_____

_____

_____

_____

_____

_____

_____

_____

WHO DOES JESUS SEE?

_____

_____

_____

_____

_____

_____

_____

_____

_____

_____

_____

_____

_____

_____

_____

_____

_____

_____

_____

_____

_____

_____

_____

_____

_____

_____

_____

What does it mean to know you are His Beloved and He delights in you?

_____

_____

_____

_____

_____

_____

_____

_____

_____

_____

_____

_____

_____

_____

_____

_____

_____

_____

_____

_____

_____

_____

_____

_____

WHO DOES JESUS SEE?

_____

_____

_____

_____

_____

_____

_____

_____

_____

_____

_____

_____

_____

_____

_____

_____

_____

_____

_____

_____

_____

_____

_____

_____

_____

_____

_____

Can you recall a moment in your life where you felt like God was saying, "I see you?"

_____

_____

_____

_____

_____

_____

_____

_____

_____

_____

_____

_____

_____

_____

_____

_____

_____

_____

_____

_____

_____

_____

WHO DOES JESUS SEE?

Chain Breakers

I am a beautiful daughter of the King!

God sees me and I am worthy of His unconditional love.

I am created in His image, and I have the mind of Christ!

Awaken & Arise

Write a thank you letter to Jesus for creating you and giving you your life. Then, in your prayer time, sit with Him and ask for a fresh encounter, a new anointing of His love, new eyes to see as He sees. Write down any pictures you get or words you hear or the feeling you get during the encounter. Remember to date this page so you can back and reference it.

_____

_____

_____

_____

_____

_____

_____

_____

_____

_____

_____

_____

_____

_____

_____

_____

_____

HEY GIRL, HE SEES YOU

PART IV

On Your Mark

"And I heard the voice of the Lord saying, 'Whom shall I send, and who will go for us?' Then I said, 'Here am I! Send me.'"
Isaiah 6:8 (MSG)

God will call You, whether you ask or not. God does have a plan, whether you care or not. The life we truly want to live, even if it may be shadowed out by all our worldly wants, is on the other side of "yes."

When I got sober, I wasn't necessarily looking for the life I've found. I wanted a way to feel better – physically, emotionally, and mentally. I knew I couldn't keep going the way I had been, but I didn't know what was ahead of me either. All I had to go on was what those other people – those nice people who lived with spiritual principles but had a history with the darker sides of life – were saying. It was a leap of faith, but it was the only choice I had. Without concrete proof, without 100% belief, and with confusion, with a little worry and doubt, I said "yes." My journey since then has been dependent on my willingness to say "yes." Each time I listen and go where I'm guided, I find another piece of God's puzzle.

Let's look at the woman who was charged with the most important assignment in the history of mankind: Mary, mother of Jesus. The beginning of her story is found in Luke 1:26 MSG.

26-28 In the sixth month of Elizabeth's pregnancy, God sent the angel Gabriel to the Galilean village of Nazareth to a virgin engaged to be married to a man descended from David. His name was Joseph, and the virgin's name, Mary. Upon entering, Gabriel greeted her:

Good morning!

You're beautiful with God's beauty,

Beautiful inside and out!

God be with you.

29-33 She was thoroughly shaken, wondering what was behind a greeting like that. But the angel assured her, "Mary, you have nothing to fear. God has a surprise for you: You will become pregnant and give birth to a son and call his name Jesus.

He will be great,

be called 'Son of the Highest.'

The Lord God will give him

the throne of his father David;

He will rule Jacob's house forever—

no end, ever, to his kingdom."

34 Mary said to the angel, "But how? I've never slept with a man."

35 The angel answered,

The Holy Spirit will come upon you,

the power of the Highest hover over you;

Therefore, the child you bring to birth

will be called Holy, Son of God.

36-38 "And did you know that your cousin Elizabeth conceived a son, old as she is? Everyone called her barren, and here she is six months pregnant! Nothing, you see, is impossible with God."

And Mary said,

Yes, I see it all now:

I'm the Lord's maid, ready to serve.

Let it be with me just as you say.

Then the angel left her.

Aside from probably being terrified at the sight of Gabriel, Mary was also confused beyond our understanding. One minute she's planning a wedding with Joseph, and in a matter of seconds, she's suddenly given the most monumental task ever given to a woman, upon which the fate of the entire human race will sit. No big deal. God knew this already though. Of course, He did!

Mary, a woman, still learning all the ways of the world, is suddenly called to raise the Messiah, the savior of the world. She had everyday worries: cleaning the clothes, preparing food, pleasing those about her. God didn't call her because of exceptional behavior, because of her socio-economic position, because of a stellar reputation, or any other trivial reason. He called her because Mary was a part of His plan all along. Our reconciliation to God is because of her willingness to say one word: yes.

Engage & Unleash

What fears do you have about saying yes?

_____

_____

_____

_____

_____

_____

_____

_____

_____

_____

_____

_____

_____

_____

_____

_____

_____

_____

_____

_____

_____

_____

_____

_____

Have you ever experienced confusion when you feel you were being led somewhere?

_____

_____

_____

_____

_____

_____

_____

_____

_____

_____

_____

_____

_____

_____

_____

_____

_____

_____

_____

_____

_____

_____

_____

_____

_____

What is a time you wish you would have said yes?

_____

_____

_____

_____

_____

_____

_____

_____

_____

_____

_____

_____

_____

_____

_____

_____

_____

_____

_____

_____

_____

_____

_____

_____

Chain Breakers

I am called!

Declarations are pretty short in this section. That's because I want you to write your own declaration(s) based on what you've learned and written about so far. You know you struggles, fears, labels, disappointments, and desires more than any other person on this earth. Write a declaration for yourself that you'll repeat for the next two weeks.

_____

_____

_____

_____

_____

_____

_____

_____

_____

_____

_____

_____

_____

_____

_____

_____

Awaken & Arise

Saying yes can be scary and intimidating but a yes can also lead to a crazy adventure with Jesus. I don't know about you, but I do not want to arrive safely at heaven's gate, but would rather slide in dirty, a little disheveled and when Jesus asks what did I do with my time I can say pull up a chair and let's chat. It has been a wild and crazy ride! So, you guessed it, this week you are going to say yes before HE even asks. Take a deep breath and pray this prayer, *God, I say yes before you even ask. Use me to be your hands and feet today in all I do and say. Thank you in advance for the encounter. I love Jesus. Amen.*

Sit and ask God what He wants you to do- what is He asking? Do you have butterflies in your stomach? Sweaty palms? That's the thing- adventure with Jesus is calling! Write it down, date it, pray over it and then yes girl go and do it! Be bold, be brave…I see a lioness arising in you, it's ok let her out. God has big plans for you, dream big! God dreams bigger!

_____

_____

_____

_____

_____

_____

_____

_____

_____

_____

_____

_____

_____

_____

_____

_____

_____

_____

_____

_____

_____

_____

_____

_____

_____

_____

_____

_____

_____

_____

_____

_____

_____

_____

_____

PART V
Get Set

See, I am doing a new thing! Now it springs up; do you not perceive it? I am making a way in the wilderness and streams in the wasteland.
Isaiah 43:19 (MSG)

We are embarking on the reality of what happens after we say "yes," have our encounter, and who we are, who we truly are, is revealed. Without filters and failure, success, and social media, without our labels and our livelihoods, who are we underneath it all and what is it like to know that through Jesus? When I had my own epiphany, I can recall not knowing exactly what to do but I did have the feeling that I wanted to get the loudest microphone commercially available to tell the entire world. No big deal! You may have already had this feeling, and if you have, welcome to the light!

My journey was almost a complete about-face from my old life. This may not be your story, but it's mine so it's the only one I can tell. I remember going and making amends for past mistakes, getting rid of all my spandex clothes that I swore made me look amazing, throwing out all of my "good" music and resetting my radio. I mean, I wasn't sure what I was doing, but I finally accepted that changing couldn't be a bad thing.

The word repent literally means to turn away from, and it just made sense that I would turn away the things in my old life. If you think this sounds overwhelming, you're right. It wasn't that I was signing up to be a Puritan. It was that I was recognizing destruction for what it was. What I put in my mind was important. What I listened to would affect my mind. What I put on myself affected the way I saw myself. Everything played a part in this revolution.

You might feel like you're in a washing machine right now. Earlier in this journey you wrote down all your labels, past hurts, and mistakes. This is who we are outside the direction of God. Make no mistake: even if you have a tight walk with the Lord, there are times we go our own way – even if it's just in our thinking. This process is still something I have to do regularly, but the first time was the heaviest. Sit still with God and ask Him for your next steps. Ask Him if making amends for the past or removing people or things from your life is what you should do. Pray for a specific direction. Write that direction down when you feel it. Sit and soak, rinse and repeat. This is not a hurry-up-and-rush-into-things moment. Let's look at some people in scripture and what steps they took.

This is the story of the woman who was crippled, found in Luke 13:10-13, MSG:

10-13 He was teaching in one of the meeting places on the Sabbath. There was a woman present, so twisted and bent over with arthritis that she couldn't even look up. She had been afflicted with this for eighteen years. When Jesus saw her, he called her over. "Woman, you're free!" He laid hands on her and suddenly she was standing straight and tall, giving glory to God.

What on Earth did this woman do after her encounter? Jesus is full of compassion for His flock. He saw her heart, her true self. In this moment, this precious moment, she can stand straight! Suddenly she can see the sky, the sun, and people's faces. She can look a friend in the eye and have a conversation because her head is no longer bent to the ground. She is whole. Whole, inside and out! There is no question; she is set completely free. In this case, this woman's next steps were literal steps. Though scripture is not explicit, we can imagine that she lifted her face; she said thank you; she walked out into the world, stumbling perhaps because it had been so long that she could do anything even close to walking. When friends asked her how this had happened, she likely shouted the praises of Jesus, her Healer.

What about Mary Magdalene who Jesus spoke to at the entrance of the tomb? Take a look at John 20, MSG:

20 1-2 Early in the morning on the first day of the week, while it was still dark, Mary Magdalene came to the tomb and saw that the stone was moved away from the entrance. She ran at once to Simon Peter and the other disciple, the one Jesus loved, gasping for breath.

"They took the Master from the tomb. We don't know where they've put him."

3-10 Peter and the other disciple left immediately for the tomb. They ran, neck and neck. The other disciple got to the tomb first, outrunning Peter. Stooping to look in, he saw the pieces of linen cloth lying there, but he didn't go in. Simon Peter arrived after him, entered the tomb, observed the linen cloths lying there, and the kerchief used to cover his head not lying with the linen cloths but separate, neatly folded by itself. Then the other disciple, the one who had gotten there first, went into the tomb, took one look at the evidence, and believed. No one yet knew from the Scripture that he had to rise from the dead. The disciples then went back home.

11-13 But Mary stood outside the tomb weeping. As she wept, she knelt to look into the tomb and saw two angels sitting there, dressed in white, one at the head, the other at the foot of where Jesus' body had been laid. They said to her, "Woman, why do you weep?"

13-14 "They took my Master," she said, "and I don't know where they put him." After she said this, she turned away and saw Jesus standing there. But she didn't recognize him.

15 Jesus spoke to her, "Woman, why do you weep?

Who are you looking for?"

She, thinking that he was the gardener, said, "Sir, if you took him, tell me where you put him so I can care for him."

16 Jesus said, "Mary."

Turning to face him, she said in Hebrew, "Rabboni!" meaning "Teacher!"

17 Jesus said, "Don't cling to me, for I have not yet ascended to the Father. Go to my brothers and tell them, 'I ascend to my Father and your Father, my God and your God.'"

18 Mary Magdalene went, telling the news to the disciples: "I saw the Master!" And she told them everything he said to her.

What an encounter! Her next steps were running! Yes, some didn't believe Mary and what she had to say. She didn't let confusion, dismay, or hurt stop her from speaking her truth. And most of us know Mary Magdalene's backstory and the labels she was given. Jesus had faith in her to follow His command. Mary Magdalene knew enough about the love Jesus had for her to follow it.

Bring it in!

We have looked at 2 different women: a woman who was healed and a woman who was hurting. The healed woman didn't ask, but Jesus showed compassion even in her silence and knew her longing to know Him. Mary Magdalene walked with Jesus and loved Him. At the tomb, she was hurting, confused, and weeping. When He revealed Himself, she was filled again with wonder and joy. Many of us have felt that. Now, we get to live her next steps, which were to run and tell the story!

It's a good time in this journey to ask yourself: What have you seen? What do you want others to "see" from your encounter?

_____

_____

_____

_____

_____

_____

_____

_____

_____

_____

_____

_____

_____

Engage & Unleash

What have you been set free from?

_____

_____

_____

_____

_____

_____

_____

_____

_____

_____

_____

_____

_____

_____

_____

_____

_____

_____

_____

_____

_____

_____

_____

_____

_____

_____

_____

_____

_____

_____

_____

_____

_____

Whatever you have encountered with Jesus is to be treasured and shared. What did you find in your encounter? What breakthrough have you received (physical, emotional, mental, spiritual)?

_____

_____

_____

_____

_____

_____

_____

_____

_____

_____

_____

_____

_____

HEY GIRL, HE SEES YOU

_____

_____

_____

What steps have you taken so far in your relationship with Him? What steps can you continue to take?

_____

_____

_____

_____

_____

_____

_____

_____

_____

_____

_____

_____

_____

_____

_____

_____

_____

_____

_____

_____

Chain Breakers

I matter to the King of Kings!

God sees me all of me and loves me right
where I'm at!

God is working all things according to His plan and I
trust His plan for my life!

May I be filled with wonders of His love and filled to
overflow with His Presence and love!

Awaken & Arise

Share your story about what Jesus has done for you with a stranger. Get out there and share your encounter with His amazing love! Pray and seek God's direction in the morning before you do this. He will open a door for you to go and share Him with others. Your story matters. You matter! Now go run, girl! Tell the story!

_____

_____

_____

_____

_____

_____

_____

_____

_____

_____

_____

_____

_____

_____

_____

_____

_____

_____

_____

PART VI

Go

Declare his glory among the nations, his marvelous works among all the peoples!
Psalms 96:3 (MSG)

We've arrived....Well, not quite. Hopefully what we've learned and felt over the course of the last few days, weeks, or months – however long this took for you – is the beginning of a new season. This is not the end. No, far from it! This is the beginning! It's imperative we understand how much we matter and how, as we embrace our identity in Him, we have His power. The only thing the enemy has is a game of distraction and deceit. In our world today, it's easy to fall into distraction. With so much mixing of reality and illusion, it's easy to be deceived. For the record, these are some of the lies you might hear whirling around your neck of the woods: you're not good enough; you don't have the right credentials; God couldn't or wouldn't use someone like you; your past is too dark; you're beyond saving; you're small; hope is for suckers.

Here are some truths you should scream in your neck of the woods: YOU are His plan A! You're not on the bench. He doesn't have a plan B. As a member of the A Team, we are to run and not grow weary, declare His glory throughout the nations, and live passionately out loud for Him!

I wanted to end with a reminder of encouragement because encouraged people encourage people. We are encouraged! Think back to the woman at the well. Remember her story? After she encounters the love and presence of Jesus, she runs into the village and tells everyone. She's so excited and so undone that she leaves her place of momentary exile and doesn't let the worry of acceptance or approval stop her from carrying out her mission. Yes, a woman of ill repute, a topic of some gossip, and a woman with a few chips on her shoulder. It's sometimes easy to overlook the context of scripture and hear a story, but not really hear a story. It's important to remember she was at the well in the middle of the day because she didn't feel worthy, loved, or equipped. Then, she was charged with carrying a message of love and hope to those who looked down on her. She epitomized God's grace, love, and mercy. The Bible is a living document in that it is still entirely relevant. There are still women at the well. There are still women who feel unworthy, unloved, and ill-equipped. God still uses these women to carry the same message she carried. So, get on up, woman!

For some of us – heck! all of us – that starts in our homes, our workplaces, our shopping trips, our girl's night out. This is where we'll run after we leave the proverbial well. Take every opportunity to share. Jesus healed and loved people who asked and those who didn't. He healed and loved people who were seeking and those who weren't. Let love lead the way in your message and your life, because love does and will always conquer all.

The first time I truly let love lead the way was in 2008. Our church was building a team to go serve in Chincha, Peru. There had been a massive earthquake and we were sending a team. Being a dental hygienist and our pastor wanting to include a dental team, I set out to fundraise and recruit a dentist for the trip. Office after office I left with a bag of supplies or money for the trip and more supplies but no commitment from a dentist. The last meeting, I had with a dentist in town I met after hours, he had a steno notebook, instruments laid out and jumped into the chair told me where to give him an injection of local anesthetic to numb the area I would be working in and then walked me through the procedures of extracting different teeth and evaluating which ones to extract. WHOA!!!!!!! Crazy right? Yep, I went home and told my husband what had just happened and the next thing I knew I was getting a passport and then was off for my first foreign mission trip to Chincha Peru with our oldest kid in tow. I remember the feeling of what in the whole wide world am I doing here God? Crying and being overwhelmed. No cell service, no home contact, a husband and three other kids at home, language barrier, tears on my face after my first patient. She gave me a hug and I cried like a baby. I shook like a tree as I administered my first injection and extracted my first tooth. A toothbrush was a luxury item, and I was way out of my comfort zone. I reminded God I didn't have a seminary degree, I was told girls don't do this, and then in the sweetest most precious voice God said, "You were created for this." I cannot express to you the feelings, the deep connection, and the sweetness of knowing in my soul like deep down in my soul that God sees me, loves me and I am important to Him. So, we could spend countless pages and I could share the crazy, amazing, miraculous, eye-opening, jaw-dropping adventures I have had the honor and privilege to be on letting love lead the way, sharing my testimony and God's love and goodness across the globe but that is for another time. But I will say this, "God does not always call the equipped but He always equips the called!"

This is the essence of "all-in living." All-in living is exactly what it sounds like. Duh. But I'll explain a little more so you can explain it to others one day. It's putting Jesus at the center of your life. He's the vine and everything else comes from the vine. If anything else is at the center of your life, your power source is cut off and things wither. All-in living is telling others your story unapologetically. Yes, this includes the dark spots when necessary. All-in living is being the Hands and Feet in your corner of the world, loving to the fullest, doing the hard work of forgiving when the opportunity pops up. All-in living is peeling off labels. All-in living is saying yes. All-in living is prayer, praise, and practice.

I want to challenge you to truly take a moment and look at what a life of all-in living looks like for YOU. Remember my story and my "all in" might look different from yours. Your passions might be different from mine. Your gifts might be different from mine. Your calling might be different from mine. But make no mistake that you have passions, gifts, and a calling. The beauty of God's creation is that we're unique. Use your gifts to glorify Him and lift up the name of Jesus in all you do and say. You are more than equipped! Jesus began with fishermen and tax collectors. His work is not finished yet.

Engage & Unleash

What does all-in living look like for you? Is there anything you need to change or make room for?

_____

_____

_____

_____

_____

_____

_____

_____

_____

_____

_____

_____

_____

_____

_____

_____
_____
_____
_____
_____
_____

Who is God calling you to share Him with?

_____
_____
_____
_____
_____
_____
_____
_____
_____
_____
_____
_____
_____
_____

_____
_____
_____

Sit with God and ask Him to reveal His gifts in you. Write these down and continue to seek deeper revelation of these gifts with Him.

_____
_____
_____
_____
_____
_____
_____
_____
_____
_____
_____
_____
_____
_____
_____
_____
_____
_____
_____
_____
_____

Chain Breakers

I am God's daughter called to reign in this life. My story matters.

I am God's mouthpiece.

God, give me words to speak as you speak, hands to do what you would do, feet to be willing to go where you ask, and eyes to see as you see. Lead the way.

Awaken & Arise

Take the list, the pictures, the gifts given by the Holy Spirit and envision putting these into action. As you look at these pictures and words in front of you ask the Holy Spirit what He would have you do and then go! Awaken and Arise! This week just say yes and allow yourself to be led by the Holy Spirit. How? You might ask- it's the quiet nudge, it is the thought of someone you haven't seen in a while so you give them a call or send a text, a smile and a God bless you, it is the wait for it- hard question Can I pray for you? And then, yes, praying! No more waiting my dear precious sister, pray and walk in all the boldness God gives you. No more chains weighing you, instead you are free to say yes and to live expecting God to reveal next steps to you as you walk in obedience. Write down that experience, date it and tell the story.

_____

_____

_____

_____

_____

_____

_____

_____

_____

_____

_____

As we wrap up, we should take time to thank God for what we've learned, what we've let go, and what we've received. We should pray for deeper truth and light so that we can carry out the purpose He's set for us. If you feel comfortable praying, you can say your own prayer. If you feel you might be a little lost about what to say, you can use this prayer.

God, I ask for a fresh anointing of Your love and Your Presence. May I live out my days completely head over head in love with you. May a deep hunger reside in me the rest of my days for the more of You. God, I ask that I walk in a newfound freedom and boldness to go and tell. Thank you, Lord! I hear your Spirit beckon me and I am ready to go wherever you call. I love you Jesus! May I never lose my wonder. Amen.

You are His beloved. You are chosen. And, hey girl, never forget that He sees you.

ABOUT THE AUTHOR

Hey there, I am married to the love of my life, Corbett. We have been blessed with four children, two daughters in love, and our first grandchild, Maxine Elizabeth. I love Jesus and my heart is happiest cheering on others to encounter their true identity in Jesus and equipping others to passionately live out all you were created to be.

When we are not working at our family business, I love grabbing every opportunity be it in our hometown of Waco, the great state of Texas (I am a proud Texan), throughout the United States or abroad, to go and be His hands and feet. I, along with our tribe, have been blessed to serve in Peru, Costa Rica, Colombia, Africa, Canada, and Haiti. We have seen miracle after miracle, healings, deliverance, and people encounter the Presence of God and fall in love with Jesus!

Sharing stories and Jesus from behind the podium or in the dirt or at a coffee shop enjoying an americano brings much joy to my heart. It is my heart song for the women of this world to embrace their true identity and encounter the overwhelming all-encompassing love of Jesus and from that place reach across the aisles, the pews, the streets, neighborhoods, work cubicles and encourage and cheer on one another in full on Jesus lovin' community. It is from this place the gates of hell shake. Get ready, join hands and let's shake the gates!

Much love-

KELLY

I love meeting new people and making new friends so look me up on our socials:

www.kellyfaulkenbery.com

Kelly Faulkenbery Facebook page

@kellyfaulkenbery Instagram

Listen weekly on the Soulstir podcast

Please send your testimony stories of breakthrough or questions to me at: kellyfaulkenbery6@gmail.com

If you would like Kelly to come and speak at your event, please send request to kellyfaulkenbery6@gmail.com